HISTORY-GEOGRAPHY
TARIH-COĞRAFYA

Karin Karakaşlı

HISTORY-GEOGRAPHY
TARIH-COĞRAFYA

*Translated from Turkish by
Sarah Howe and Canan Marasligil*

First published in 2017
by The Poetry Translation Centre Ltd
2 Wardrobe Place, London EC4V 5AH

www.poetrytranslation.org

Poems © Karin Karakaşlı 2012–2015

Translations from the Turkish © Sarah Howe
apart from 'History-Geography', 'Ontological Distance' and 'Washing Lines'
© The Poetry Translation Centre
Introduction © Canan Marasligil

The Turkish poems included this chapbook were first published in two separate
collections by Karin Karakaşlı: *Her Kimsen Sana* (Aras Yayıncılık, 2012)
and İrtifa Kaybı (Aras Yayıncılık, 2015)

ISBN: 978-0-9575511-8-3

A catalogue record for this book is available from the British Library

Designed in Minion by Libanus Press
Printed by F.E. Burman Ltd
Print production by Rubine Solutions Ltd

The Poetry Translation Centre is supported using public funding by
Arts Council England

Contents

Introduction	6
History-Geography	9
Feather	11
Fluorescent	13
Galata	15
Succour	19
Deserted	21
Uniform	23
Strategic	25
Purple Red	29
Dripstone	31
Q&A	33
Ontological Distance	35
Juniper Prayer Beads	37
Washing Lines	39
About the authors	40

Introduction

Karin Karakaşlı is an Armenian-Turkish poet who lives in Istanbul and writes in Turkish. As well as poetry she pens regular columns and opinion pieces for independent media outlets, and writes fiction, non-fiction and children's literature.

The deep pain and scars left by Turkey's negationist state discourse on the Armenian genocide of 1915 are visible throughout Karakaşlı's oeuvre and are omnipresent in her poetry. The Turkish state's continual suppression of the forming of a common memory affects people not only of Armenian descent but from many communities such as the Greeks and the Kurds. This denial is an example of how, government after government, those in power in Turkey have consistently erased the history of whole parts of their population. It is in this context of past and present violations of basic rights, freedoms of expression and human dignity that Karin Karakaşlı seeks to exist with her poetry.

The poems in this chapbook have been selected from two poetry collections: *Her Kimsen Sana / Whoever You Are, (This Is) For You* (2012) and *İrtifa Kaybı / Loss of Altitude* (2015). They reflect the intense and painful emotions buried deep in the soul of the poet, and in the souls of many people in Turkey.

> *No one is the first to set foot on any soil*
> *You're always borne by souls who passed before*

These two lines from the title poem 'History-Geography' are characteristic of how Karakaşlı addresses painful historical and cultural issues in a powerfully economical way. Turkey as a nation has denied the Armenians and others their right to mourn collectively, and so the memories lost to this part of the population are also lost to the Turkish people as a whole, whose collective memory lacks these painful but necessary narratives.

The national propensity towards erasing stories that disturb official narratives has taken its toll on Turkey's politics, its economic growth and even its natural environment, as Karakaşlı illustrates in 'Strategic', a sorrowful account of her relationship with a salt cedar.

Karakaşlı's pain can be deeply felt in most of her poems. However alongside this we encounter an enormous amount of love for the geography she lives in, especially the city of Istanbul. Karakaşlı has an almost synergetic relationship with this city (as we can read in her poem 'Galata') – with the history embedded in every stone, every building and every landscape.

There is a constant struggle in Turkey between being oneself and having to fit into a mould – a mould shaped by nationalistic values and imposed by a majority – which makes daily life extremely difficult for people who come from one of the many minority communities. This state of struggle and in-betweenness is described in the poem 'Uniform' – from school days dressed in 'mouse grey' skirts all the way to adulthood.

The poet holds a mirror to society, one which is not always welcome – as is clearly expressed in these three lines from 'Purple Red':

Now I am naked in the middle of a crowd
A naked mirror they will gaze into
and hate their own reflection

Many lines in Karakaşlı's poems open up our thoughts to wider issues we all face across our many geographies. Such as these from the poem 'Strategic':

We call a mass lie the new truth
Hypocrisy is going legitimate.

These lines may mean different things to different people. For instance, here Karakaşlı refers to the denial of the Armenian genocide, but also to the ongoing lies told by corrupt governments – a message which will no doubt resonate globally.

The human suffering, the yearning for love and hope, portrayed in Karakaşlı's poems is the daily reality for people in many parts of the world. Beyond specific historical and cultural contexts, Karin Karakaşlı's poetry is a beautiful expression of the human soul: with all its darkness and light, including all the many shades of emotions and thoughts in between, seeking to build a common language through poetry.

Canan Marasligil

Tarih-Coğrafya

Kimse ilk basmaz bir toprağa
Sırtlanırsın geçmiş ruhları
Tanrılar Tanrıçalar da bir
zaman sen gibi canlardı
İçinden geçer hepsinin gücü, zaafı
Aşağıda toprağın üzerinde
kafilelerce çoğaldı
ölü ölümlüler
Gıkları çıkmadı
Allah'ın unuttuğunu kimse anımsamadı

Tarihimsin bir miktar kabul
ama coğrafyam değil
Yer kaplayanların adıdır coğrafya
ve kalmak yürek ister

Ölülerimle kaldım coğrafyamda
Sen kendini inkâr ettin
resmî oldun, hakikatinden boşaldıkça

Hayatımla kaldım coğrafyamda
kendi tarihimi yazmaya

History-Geography

No one is the first to set foot on any soil
You're always borne by souls who passed before
Time was, gods and goddesses
were alive just like you
Their strengths and weaknesses flow through you
into the earth
trodden underfoot by the procession
of the mortal dead

Granted some of you are my history
yet not my geography
Geography is the name of those who occupy the land
and it takes heart to stay

I stayed in my geography with my dead
Yet you denied your very self
Turned official, emptied of truth

I stayed in my geography with my life
to write my own history

Tüy

Ne kadar ağır değil mi
bir tüyü kaldırmak
Tutmak ellerinin arasında
bırakmamak
ne büyük bir iş
Cünkü tüy, uçanın emaneti sana
başka tür bir hayatın kehaneti
ve bakma, aslında her kehanet de
bir iç bilgi teyidi

Bir hacıyatmaz noktası var omurgamda
vuruyorlar savruluyorum
ama düşmüyorum nispet gibi
sil baştan başlıyor hayat
bir ileri bir geri

Tepeden bir tüy süzülüyor
görünürde kuş yok, bir kendi gelmiş
bana konmaya
Bilirim, tüyler bana melek işareti
Tutuyorum ellerimin arasında
hayat gibi

Feather

How heavy it is
to lift a feather
Laid across two palms
not letting it drop
What a weighty task
For this feather, entrusted to you by a creature of flight
portends another kind of life
but don't be fooled, in truth, any portent
only confirms what you know inside

There is a wobbly point on my spine
they are hitting me I sway
but obstinate I do not fall
life starts up again at the beginning
one step forward one step back

From overhead floats down a feather
not a bird in sight, it came on its own
to perch on me
Feathers, I know, are signs sent to me by angels
I cup them in my hands
like life

Fosforlu

Martıların fosforlu göründüğü
akşam saatlerini bilir misin?
İlle soğuktur ve irkiltici
Floresan ışığı gibi
çiğ ve çirkin olursun sanki
aykırı ve iğreti

Telaşlı insanların çantalarını yersin
böğrüne, dönüp bakmazlar
Yaprak ve kâğıt dolu yol kenarları
Durmak bir onların hakkı

Gidecek bir yerin olmalı
Girecek bir kapın
Salınanı sevmiyorlar, yol
illa bir yere varmalı

Kimsenin göğe baktığı yok
martıların fosforlu göründüğü
akşam saatleri

Fluorescent

Those evening hours
when the seagulls seem to glow like neon
Inescapably startling and cold
Like a fluorescent tube
showing you as though newly raw and ugly
incongruous and shoddy

The bags of rushing passers-by will strike
you in the side, they won't look back
Roadsides clogged with leaves and paper
Only they have the right to stop

You need a place to go
A door to enter
People here don't like wanderers, the road
must lead somewhere

No one looks up at the sky
those evening hours
when the seagulls seem to glow like neon

Galata

Bir kuleye sevdalıyım
Gece vakti ekseninde
mıknatıslı gibi dönenen
fosforlu beyaz martılardanım

Bir kadraja sığdık siyah-beyaz
Uzatmalı sonbahardı serin ve ışıklı
Sevdalım heybetliydi
taş ve kökten uzun bir hikâye, sonu hep
bende bitti

Alışkanlık olmuştu vapurda başımı kaldırıp
onu arıyordum, oradaysa daha
sıramı sayıyordum

Zordu tabii ne sandınız
bu şehirde öğütülmeden tek parça kalabilmek
her şey yıkılırken
zamansızca ayakta kalan bir oydu
Ve ona baktıkça sorardım kendime, sahi
benim kalbim niye hep böyle toydu
ki biz buna kısaca enayilik diyorduk
aramızda ve gözümüzden yaş gelene kadar
gülüyorduk

Rüzgârın kulesi derdim ona
En tepede insan, bulutlara komşu
İstanbul fır dönerdi etrafında dolandıkça
Yüzyıllarca öncenin taşları kayardı
bugünün yağmurunda

Galata

I am in love with a tower
I am one of the fluorescent white seagulls
spinning like magnets
round its axis by night

We squeezed into a black and white shot
It was an extended autumn, cool and light
My beloved was majestic
A story older than stone and roots, at the end
of the last chapter I was always there

It became a habit, I would lift up my head on the ferry
to look for the tower, check it was still there
I would pay homage

Of course it was a challenge to stay in one piece
in this city, not to be pounded, what did you expect?
Out of its time, the tower was the only thing left standing
when everything else came crashing down
And as I gazed at it, I asked myself
why my heart was always so naïve
a fool, to be blunt, as we'd call it between ourselves
till our eyes swam with tears
and we were laughing

I would call it the tower of the wind
The person at the summit, neighbour to the clouds
Istanbul would spin round it in devoted circles
The stones of past centuries would slip
with today's rain

'Gökyüzünü Galata'ya indirip
bir ömür yaşayalım mı?'
diye bir duvar yazısı
bana sorsun isterdim yazan her kimse
önünden her geçtiğimde

Kollarımı açıp sarıldım
Taştan sevgili ısındı avuçlarımda

'Shall we lower the sky to Galata
and live forever?'
said a snatch of graffiti
and I wanted its author to ask me
every time I walked past

I opened my arms to embrace it
My stone beloved grew warm between my palms

Medet

Seni medet bildim ben
Nedenini sorma
sadece yardım et

Peçetedeki şarap lekesi
gibi dağılmışım
Ama hep koyu kırmızıyım
kıvamlı, buruk, ıslak

Kaldırım taşına fırlatılan bilyeler
gibi dağılmışım
renkli, çocuksu, parlak

Sahaflara düşen eski aile fotoğrafları
gibi dağılmışım
asil, eski ve biraz ağlak

Çanta gibi toparlanamıyor kalp dediğin
Oda gibi düzenlenemiyor zihin
O yüzden diyeceğim o ki
yardım et sadece
sorma nedenini

Medet bildim ben seni

Succour

I always took you for succour
Don't ask why
just help me

Like wine bleeding across a napkin
I splattered
But I am ever a dark red
thick, sour, wet

Like marbles strewn across paving stones
I scattered
colourful, childish, bright

Like old family photos wound up in second-hand bookshops
I tattered
noble, old and a bit tearful

This thing you call heart can't be tidied like a purse
The mind can't be rearranged like a room
That's why I will say
just help me
don't ask why

You I always took for succour

Tenha

Okumadığım gazetelerin sayfalarından aktı gün
tıka basa söz, fazla resim
Söyleyeceğimi unutunca söylediğim de
siliniyor hafızadan
Günlerin adı olması ne komik
hepsi bir sonsuzlukta asılı kaldıkça

Ne sandın ya
Her dil bir veda aslında
Her dil çoklu çaresizlik

Masumiyet büyük kaçıyor ağzına
küçük bedenleri tüketen Çin
mallarını aldığında
Kâinat düşlemiştin sahi
Hayat Made in China

Sınav çözen sınıf sessizliğindeyim
Bir şey vardı unuttum
ya da çekindim paylaşmaya

Karanlık bir sarnıç var kalbimde
Dışım nasıl kalabalık
içim nasıl tenha

Deserted

The day flows past the newspaper spreads I leave unread
crammed with words, a surfeit of images
Whenever I forget what I was about to say, even what I do speak
is wiped from memory
Isn't it funny how some days are given titles
all hanging there in eternity

What did you expect
Every language is really a goodbye
Every language is a manifold despair

Innocence is too big for your mouth
China consumes small bodies
every time you buy its goods
Yes, you dreamed of a universe
Life is Made in China

I'm silent as a classroom mid-exam
There was something I forgot
or was too shy to share

In my heart there is a dark and vaulted well
How crowded I am on the outside
how deserted within

Sivil

Ne etsen bir şeye benzemez
okul etekleri
Üstten kıvırdığında da
daralttığında da değişmez
Hep o aynı faremsi gri

Çabalı farklılık nedir bilirsin
Kaç kuşak sonrasında
Biraz da genç kızlığındır
baktığın, evcil deli

Hâlâ zor sivil zamanlar
Ve çok sefil bir gayret
Kendi olmak dediğin

İlk darbendir gri okul etekleri

Uniform

They won't look good no matter what you do
school skirts
Even when you roll them up at the waist
or take them in it makes no difference
Always that same mouse grey

You know the pains it takes to look different
After so many generations
It's a piece of your girlhood
you're looking at, that half-tamed madness

Even now moments out of uniform are hard
And it demands a miserable effort
What we call being oneself

It's their first strike against us
the grey school skirt

Stratejik konum

Bir ılgın ağacıyla tanışmıştım
Deniz kıyısında haşmetli neşeli
bir yeşildi
Çok oturmuşluğum dertleşmişliğim var onunla
Güngörmüş pürtüklü gövdesini
okşar, hışırtılı dallarına bırakırdım
kimselere söyleyemediklerimi
Şehre dönmeden sarılır helalleşir
Bir sonraki yaza görüşmek üzere derdik

Sonraki yaz geldiğimde denizde
bir boşluk vardı
Neyi eksik bilemedim önce
Derken bir baktım ılgınımı
budamışlar ortasından
Deniz manzarasını kesmesin diye

Bana görünmek istemedi ılgın elletmedi
kendini çünkü dalı kalmayınca
gövdesini yaprak basmıştı ve
güzelim üst dalları artık küskün
sarı çırpılardı

Denizi öyle sevmişler ki ağacına kıymışlar
Sahip olacaksan bir şeye geri kalanı engeldir
Stratejik konumun yanlışsa
Bedel ödetirler duruşuna
Ilgın ne bilsin bunları

Sevmek ne tuhaf ne acıklı bir kelime

Strategic

I met a salt cedar
by the sea
It was a cheerful stately green
I sat with it and shared my troubles many times
caressing its rough, wise trunk
To its rustling branches I would trust
all the things I couldn't tell
Before my return to the city we embraced, bid farewell
Till next summer, we said

The next summer I came to the sea
there was an emptiness
At first I didn't realise what was missing
Then I saw my salt cedar
split down the middle
obscuring the sea view no longer

The salt cedar didn't want me to see it, to let me touch
the spots bared of branches
Its hollowed trunk filled with leaves
and its beautiful upper boughs now disconsolate
yellow limbs

So much did they love the sea they sacrificed its only tree
In the quest to possess something, everything else becomes pure obstacle
If your strategy means standing in the wrong position
you'll be made to pay the price
How could the salt cedar know all this

What a strange and painful word is love

Denizin başladığı yerde duruyorum
Kum ıslak ve yoğun
Tabanımın şeklini alıyor bastığım yerde
Ama denizin o sıfır noktasında
Hiçbir iz kalıcı değil
Bir cilveli hareketle siliverir beni

İnsanların birbirinin yüzüne nal izi
bıraktığı bir şehirdenim
Hepimizin elinin altında buz
torbaları ve hücre yenileyici kremler
Geceler o izleri okşamakla
Gündüzler saklamakla geçiyor
Toplu yalana yeni gerçeklik diyoruz
Riya meşruiyet kazanıyor

Hep bir kayıp hep bir eksilme duygusu
var. Sanki bir şeylerini
çaldılar, sen hiç bilemedin
Adını koymadıkça kendinden eksildin
Koca aşklar matruşkalara ufalandı
Ne zamandır yetiyor sevdiklerine
'Sen de artık herkes gibisin' kalıbı
Gerisi hep o aynı irtifa kaybı

I'm standing where the sea begins
The sand is wet and thick
It takes the shape of my sole where I step
But at this zero point of the sea
No trace is permanent
It will erase me with one coquettish flick

I come from a city where
people leave horseshoe welts on other people's faces
At our fingertips we all have ice
packs and cell renewal creams
Nights go by caressing those scars
Days spent hiding them
We call a mass lie the new truth
Hypocrisy is going legitimate

There is always a sense of loss, always a sense
of being diminished. As though something of yours
were stolen, but you had no idea
The longer it went unnamed the more you lost a part of yourself
A vast love story dwindled down to matryoshka dolls
Since when is the 'You're like everyone else now' mould
enough for the ones you love
What's left is always the same old loss of altitude

Mor kırmızı

Habire düşerdim, sanki göremediğim birileri
çelmelerdi ayaklarımı
Çok ağrırdı bacaklarım
hep çürük hep mor
Habire sol elimi keserdim bir de
Suyun altında yanardı kesik yeri
hep kan hep kırmızı

Habire yanılırdım en kötüsü
Fazla kıymet, emanet giysi gibi
dururdu güvendiklerimde
'O ama çok farklı' dediklerimde
Öğrendim zamanla, bütün farklar aynıdır

Ruhum gururundan morarırdı
ve yüzüm kızarırdı utancından
Çocukken battaniyeden çadır
yapardım ya hani sığınmaya
Şimdi çıplaktım insanların ortasında
Çıplak ayna, görür
ve nefret ederlerdi yansımalarından

O yüzden geriye kalan sadece
iki tayfı gökkuşağı kaderimin
hep mor hep kırmızı

Ne edeyim, söylemek zorundayım
Çok aldatıldım fazla bıçaklandım
hep mosmor hep kankırmızı

Purple Red

I kept falling, as if people I couldn't see
were tripping me up
My legs hurt a lot
always bruised always purple
And I kept cutting my left hand too
The gash burned under the water
always blood always red

Worst case I would always be mistaken
Too much esteem hung like borrowed
clothes on those I trusted
When they said 'But she's quite different'
I learned in time, all differences are alike

My soul was bruised by pride
and my face flushed with shame
When I was a kid I'd build a tent out of a blanket
to take refuge in, you know
Now I am naked in the middle of a crowd
A naked mirror they will gaze into
and hate their own reflection

And that's why the only thing still left
is the spectacular twin rainbows of my fate
always purple always red

What can I do, I have no choice but to say it
So often I've been deceived, stabbed too many times
always deep purple always blood red

Damlataşı

Gözyaşını büyütünce
damlataşı olur mu?
Hani şu mağarada on beş yıl
damla damla akıp donan
Donup akan

Taş nasıl da yaşıyor şaşarsın
Damlataşından sarkıtlarla kaplı
bir mağarada gördüm taşın kalbini
Damla damla atıyor, büyüyordu
Dokunmamız yasaktı, insan eli
hep şifalı değil
Avuçtaki ter salgısı
katiliymiş damla taşının
Parmak değince duruyor
Taşlaşıyor öylece

Avucumun terlediği birileri
de benim katilimdi bir vakit
Aşkımı akıtırken damla damla
Sarktığım
        Taşlaştığım
                Damladan
                        Kırıldım

Dripstone

When tears grow bigger
do they become dripstones?
You know, like in those caves after fifteen years
dripping drop by drop and freezing
Frozen as they flow

You'd be surprised at how that stone lives
In a cave lined with dripstone stalactites
I have seen the heart of the stone
Drop by drop it was beating, growing
Touching was forbidden, the human hand
doesn't always heal
The sweat pricking from our palms
will prove in fact the stone's killer
When the finger touches it
It will petrify just like that

Someone sweating against my palm
once was my killer too
As my love flowed out drop after drop
from the stone
           where I'd hung
                    frozen
                            I broke

Anket

en vazgeçilmez uyuşturucu: yalan
en gerçekçi bitki: kaktüs
en eski yerleşim ilkesi: talan
en etkili botoks maddesi: gamsızlık
en yalnız yer: sırtın ortası
en sıcak kap: çaydanlık
en sakin beklenti: balık oltası
en zorlu coğrafya: kalp
en zalim terör örgütü: aşk
en büyük işkence: umut
en zorlu taşıma aracı: tabut

Q & A

the most indispensable drug: a lie
the most realistic plant: a cactus
the oldest principle of settlement: plunder
the most effective Botox ingredient: lightheartedness
the loneliest place: the middle of the back
the hottest vessel: a kettle
the calmest expectancy: a fishing rod
the most challenging geography: the heart
the cruellest terrorist organisation: love
the greatest torture: hope
the toughest form of transport: the coffin

Ontolojik Mesafe

Gördüğünde beni, bir adım geri dur
koruyalım ontolojik mesafemizi
Olur ya, kendine yenilirsin
ruhunun gerçeğine
direnemezsin sonra
Oysa bahaneler için
hep mesafe lazım
Suçlamak ve sorumluluk atmak için
Topun yuvarlanmasına alan
unutulmaya zaman lazım
Geri dur bir adım beni gördüğünde
Ontolojik mesafemizi koruyalım

Ontological Distance

When you see me, take a step back
let's keep our ontological distance
Who knows, you might be defeated by yourself
by the truth of your soul
and you'll never get over it
To make excuses
you always need some distance
To accuse and to blame
the ball needs room to roll
and we need time to forget
Take a step back when you meet me
our ontological distance must be kept

Andiz Tespih

Kokusunu içine çek, rahatla, beni hatırla dedi
arkadaşım elime andız tespihi tutuştururken
Onu burnuma götürmek bir anlık yolculuk
Andız ağacı tohumu nasıl cömert
Kırmızı şarabın tanelenmiş hali gibi
içinden parlak ve kıvamlı
Parmaklarımın arasından aktıkça
rayihasını bırakıyor peşi sıra
Eski zaman kilise kokusu bu
Bir nevi buhurdanlık

İki Cizvit rahip beliriyor ben taneleri okşadıkça
Gonca güllü cam vazo, Meryem Ana sunağı
melek bibloları, sonra kan çok kan
çünkü rahipler itina ile öldürülür ülkemde
Katil "ahlâksız teklifte bulundu" der
Hep on sekizinden gün almamıştır
ben bir günde birkaç yaş büyüdükçe

Andız ağacı tohumu nasıl sert
Dökülen kanın tanelenmiş hali gibi
oluk ılık oluk ılık
aktıkça parmaklarımın arasından
gözüm kararıyor gitgide
Hep yürütürler seni zaten
hep asla varamayacağın bir yere
menzilsiz istikamete

Sonrası mı sonrası yok
sonrası mezarsız ölüm
tırın arkasında ya da yolcu teknesinde
yığılı malmışçasına üstüste bindirilen
yeni bir hayat diye en eski ölümü ölen
göçmenler gibi

Sonrası mı sonrası yok
Sonrası istatistik sonrası flaş haber
Andız tespihe sığmaz devlet elli ölümler

Juniper Prayer Beads

Inhale their smell, relax, remember me
said my friend pushing the prayer beads into my hand
Lifting them to my nose is a moment's journey
How generous the seed of the juniper tree
Like red wine dried to grains
bright and full-bodied from within
Pouring through my fingers
they leave behind their lovely scent
This is the fragrance of the ancient church
incense trailing from a censer

As I stroke the beads two Jesuit priests appear
Glass vase with rose buds, Mother Mary's altar
angel trinkets, then blood so much blood
because priests are killed with care in my country
The murderer would say "it was an immoral promise that he spread"
He wasn't yet eighteen
while I age years in a single day

How hard the seed of the juniper tree
Like spilled blood dried to grains
lukewarm gutter lukewarm gutter
pouring through my fingers
Eyes dimming I stagger more and more
Still they make you walk
always towards a place you will never reach
a destination without respite

As for after well there is no after
after is a graveless death
in the back of a truck or a passenger boat
stacked like goods piled on top of other goods
like migrants
dying the oldest of deaths as if it were a new life

As for after well there is no after
After is a statistic after is breaking news
Murder at the hands of the state prayer beads can't contain

Çamaşır İpleri

Yarın yeni değil
Bir bitmeyen bugünde
asılı hayat
Soluk mavi mandallarla
tutturulmuş umudum
Pas izi kalmasın diye
habire omuz başlarıma bakıyorum

Güneşe asılmış çamaşırlar
gibi olmayı isterdim
ak pak mis ferah
rüzgârla oynaşmayı
Ama bazen yaptığından utandırıyorlar
Havada kalınca uzattığın el
boşluk kanatıyor avucumu
İsa'nın yaraları da çividen değil
ihanetten, anlıyor oluyorum

Yine de bırakıyorum kendimi
bir kez daha tesadüfe
güzele şaşırmaya
Lavanta değil beyaz sabun kokuyorum
gecenin sabahında

Washing Lines

Tomorrow is not new
Life is suspended
on a today without end
My hope hangs
from faded blue clothespegs
I keep checking the shoulders
to stop rust stains from forming

I wish I could be like
washing hung out in the sun
spick and span and fresh and clean
fondled by the wind
Yet sometimes they make you feel ashamed
The outstretched hand not taken
an emptiness that makes my palm bleed
Now I know the stigmata were caused
not by nails but by betrayal

And yet, once again,
I give myself up to happenstance
to be surprised by beauty
As dawn breaks
I smell soap, not lavender

KARIN KARAKAŞLI was born in Istanbul in 1972. She graduated in Translation and Interpreting Studies. From 1996 to 2006 she worked at the Turkish-Armenian weekly newspaper *Agos* as editor, head of the editorial department and columnist. She has an MA in Comparative Literature, and has worked as a translation instructor at the university and as a teacher of Armenian language and literature in an Armenian High School. Her work was included in the 2010 story collection, *The Book of Istanbul* (Comma Press, UK). In 2014 some of her poems were published in a major anthology of world poems, *My Voice*, published by the Poetry Translation Centre.

SARAH HOWE is a British poet, academic and editor. Her first book, *Loop of Jade* (Chatto & Windus, 2015), won the T.S. Eliot Prize and The Sunday Times / PFD Young Writer of the Year Award, and was shortlisted for the Forward Prize for Best First Collection. She has performed her work at festivals internationally and on BBC Radio 3 and 4. Her previous fellowships include a Research Fellowship at Gonville and Caius College, Cambridge, a Hawthornden Fellowship, the Harper-Wood Studentship and a Fellowship at Harvard University's Radcliffe Institute. She is currently a Leverhulme Fellow in English at University College London.

CANAN MARAŞLIGIL is a freelance writer, literary translator, editor and curator based in Amsterdam. She specialises in contemporary Turkish literature as well as in comics. Her interest is in challenging official narratives and advocating freedom of expression through a wide range of creative projects and activities. Canan has worked with cultural organisations across wider Europe and has participated in a range of residencies at the Free Word Centre in London (2013), at WAAW in Senegal (2015), at Copenhagen University (2015) and at La Contre Allée in Lille (2017). She is the creator of 'City in Translation', a project exploring languages and translation in urban spaces.